BASICS OF C#.NET PROGRAMMING LANGUAGE

SOLUTIONS FOR .NET QUESTIONS

KINNARI V. MISHRA

This book is dedicated to those students and teachers who are willing to learn about the basic concept of C#.Net Programming Language to create their own applications like console and windows application.

Contents

FOREWORD

If you want to learn any language and you are willing to create any program or application you need to clear your basic concepts of that particular programming language. The .Net Programming language is useful to create many applications as well as web services.The visual studio is provide you the platform to create different types of application using different languages.Microsoft visual studio provides you more than 80 languages to create your application.

C# is part of the language which is provided by visual studio. By using C#.Net you are able to create different applications like Console,Windows,Web application,Web services and also can create mobile application.But if you wants to create mobile application in visual studio for that you have to install xamarian framework. After installing the framework you have to add namespace.

This book fully embraces the potential of C#.Net to empower its users.It's friendly and approachable text intended help you level up not just your knowledge of .Net,but also you reach the confidence as a programmer in general. So dive in and get ready to learn - and welcome to the C#.Net programming language community.

- Kinnari Mishra

PREFACE

This book is for computer scientists,computer engineers and others who wants to learn and create better programs using .Net programming language.

Our aim is to explain the enduring concepts underlying all computer system, and to show you the concrete ways that these ideas affect the correctness, performance, and utility of your application programs.This book is written from a programmer's perspective, describing how application programmers can use their knowledge of a system to write better programs.

If you study and learn the concepts in this book, you will be on your way to becoming the rare "power programmer" who knows how things work and how to fix them. Our aim is to present the fundamental concepts in ways that you will find useful right away. You will also be prepared to studying such topics as C#.net applications like console,windows application using ADO.Net.

Acknowledgements

I would like to express my greatest appreciation to the all individuals who have helped and supported me throughout writing this book.I am thankful to my family members and my colleagues during this book writing from initial advice, and encouragement, which led to the final completion of the book.

I special acknowledgement goes to my motivator Mrs. Hetal Bhaidasna who helped me in completing the book by exchanging interesting ideas and sharing their experience. I would like to thank my husband Mr.Vijay Mishra and my brother Mr.AjayKumar Tripathi who always motivated me to do best in my career.

I wish to thank my parents as well for their undivided support and interest who inspired me and encouraged me to go my own way, without whom I would be unable to complete this book.

At the end, I want to thank my friends who displayed appreciation to my work and motivated me to continue my work.

- **Kinnari Mishra**

PROLOGUE

In this book the basic details of C#.Net programming language is given and it is starting from the architecture of .Net Programming language which explains that how it works and how your program will execute from MSIL code to native code. C#.net is a Event driven programming language which is based on the events given by the user.

Before learning the concepts of .net you should have the basic knowledge of object oriented programming language. C#.Net is a powerful,Simple and Pure Object Oriented Programming language.

It has different versions can exist side by side.It is also Type safe and provides rich libraries of many built in functions.

Using C# we can create iOS,Android and windows phone native applications but for that you need to install xamarian framework.

I

Basics of C#.Net Programming Language

•

Explain .NET Architecture with its Diagram.

Net Framework is a software development platform developed by Microsoft for building and running Windows applications. The .Net framework consists of developer tools, programming languages, and libraries to build desktop and web applications. It is also used to build websites, web services, and games.

Microsoft visual studio provides more than 80+ languages to craete application.

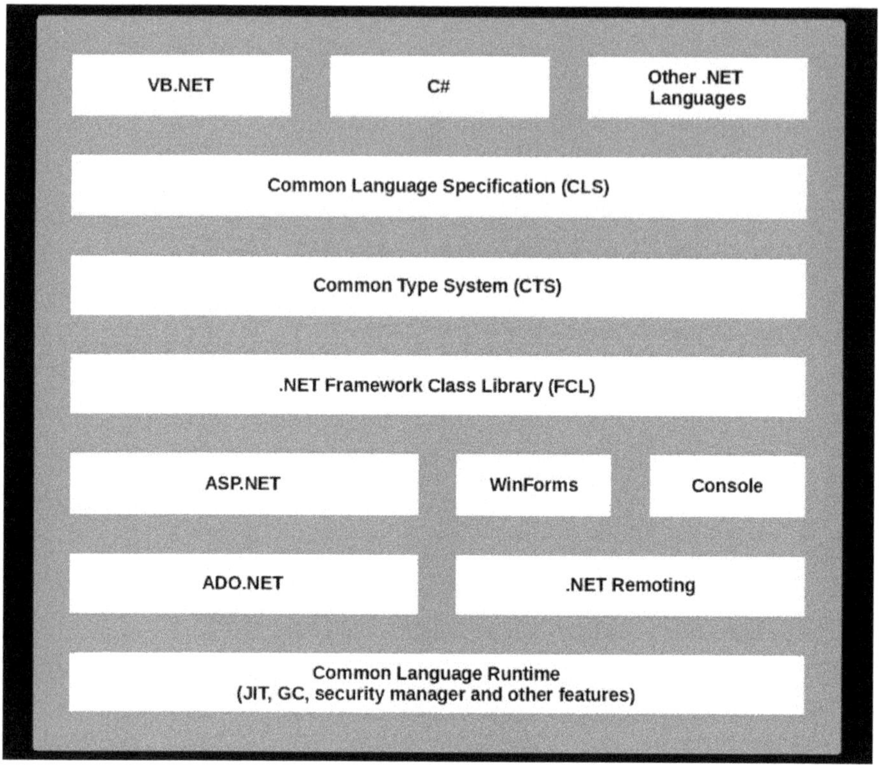

VB.NET
C#
Other .NET Languages
Common Language Specification (CLS)
Common Type System (CTS)
.NET Framework Class Library (FCL)
ASP.NET
WinForms
Console
ADO.NET
.NET Remoting
Common Language Runtime
(JIT, GC, security manager and other features)

.Net Architecture

Net Framework Architecture is a programming model for the .Net platform that provides an execution environment and integration with various programming languages for simple development and deployment of various Windows and desktop applications. It consists of class libraries and reusable components.

Components of .Net Framework:

The architecture of .Net framework is based on the following key components.

1. CLR - Common Language Runtime:

The "Common Language Infrastructure" or CLI is a platform in .Net architecture on which the .Net programs are executed.

The CLI has the following key features:

Exception Handling – Exceptions are errors which occur when the application is executed.

Examples of exceptions are:

- If an application tries to open a file on the local machine, but the file is not present.
- If the application tries to fetch some records from a database, but the connection to the database is not valid.

Garbage Collection – Garbage collection is the process of removing unwanted resources when they are no longer required.

Examples of garbage collection are

- A File handle which is no longer required. If the application has finished all operations on a file, then the file handle may no longer be required.
- The database connection is no longer required. If the application has finished all operations on a database, then the database connection may no longer be required.

Working with Various programming languages –

- **Language** – The first level is the programming language itself, the most common ones are VB.Net and C#.
- **Compiler** – There is a compiler which will be separate for each programming language. So underlying the VB.Net language, there will be a separate VB.Net compiler. Similarly, for C#, you will have another compiler.
- **Common Language Interpreter** – This is the final layer in .Net which would be used to run a .net program developed in any programming language. So the subsequent compiler will send the program to the CLI layer to run the .Net application.

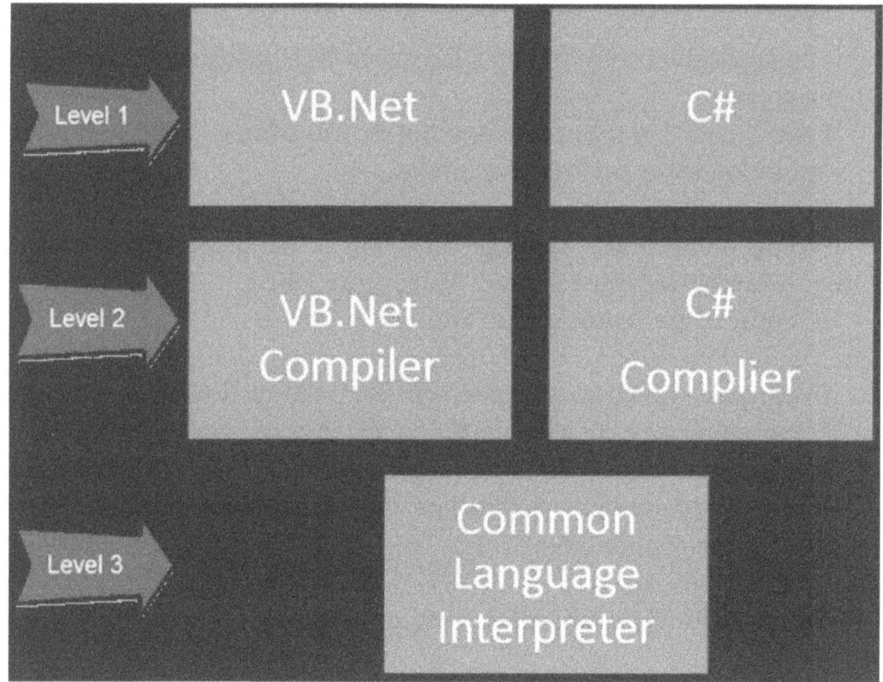

Common Language Interpreter

2. Class Library

The .NET Framework includes a set of standard class libraries. A class library is a collection of methods and functions that can be used for the core purpose.

For example, there is a class library with methods to handle all file-level operations. So there is a method which can be used to read the text from a file. Similarly, there is a method to write text to a file.

Most of the methods are split into either the System.* or Microsoft.* namespaces. (The asterisk * just means a reference to all of the methods that fall under the System or Microsoft namespace)

A namespace is a logical separation of methods. We will learn these namespaces more in detail in the subsequent chapters.

Sample Rules:

1. Representation of text strings
2. Internal representation of enumerations

3. Definition of static members and this is a subset of the CTS which all .NET languages are expected to support.

4. Microsoft has defined CLS which are nothing but guidelines that language to follow so that it can communicate with other .NET languages in a seamless manner.

•

Describe the role for CLR

CLR (Common Language Runtime) is basic component of .NET Framework. It provides an environment to run .NET applications on targeted machine. CLR provides environment for all .NET languages compilers for converting source code into a common language known as **IL** or **MSIL** or **CIL**.

CLR provides multiple services to execute processes, like memory management service and security services. CLR performs multiple tasks to manage the execution of .NET applications. **Following responsibilities of CLR are given below:**

1. Automatic memory management
2. Code access security
3. Garbage collection
4. JIT compilation

1) Automatic memory management

CLR calls various predefined functions of .NET framework to allocate and de-allocate memory of .NET objects. So that, developers need not to write code to explicitly allocate and de-allocate memory.

2) Code access security

CLR allows access to code to perform only those tasks for that it has permission. It also checks user's permissions using authentication and configuration files of .NET applications.

3) Garbage collection

GC is used to prevent memory leaks or holes. Garbage collector of CLR automatically determines the best time to free the memory, which is allocated to an object for execution.

4) JIT compilation

JIT stands for Just In Time. It is also an important part of Common Language Runtime (CLR), JIT compiler converts MSIL code to targeted machine code for execution.

•

List out the features of .NET programming language.

Following are the features of .Net Programming.

1. Common Executive Environment:-

All .NET applications run under a common execution environment, called the Common Language Runtime. The CLR facilitates the interoperability between different .NET languages such as C#, Visual Basic, Visual C++, etc. by providing a common environment for the execution of code written in any of these languages.

2. Common Type System:-

The .NET framework follows types of systems to maintain data integrity across the code written in different .NET compliant programming languages. CTS ensures that objects of the programs that are written in different programming languages can communicate with each other to share data.

CTS prevents data loss when a type in one language transfers data to its equivalent type in one language transfer data to its equivalent type in other languages. For example, CTS ensures that data is not lost while transferring an integer variable of visual basic code to an integer variable of C# code.

The common type system CTS defines a set of types and rules that are common to all languages targeted at the CLR. It supports both value and reference types. Value types are created in the stack and include all primitive types, structs, and enums. In contrast, reference types are created in the managed heap and include objects, arrays, collections, etc.

3. Multi-language support:-

.NET provides multi-language support by managing the compilers that are used to convert the source to intermediate language (IL) and from IL to native code, and it enforces program safety and security.

The basis for multiple language support is the common type system and metadata. The basic data types used by the CLR are common to all languages. There are therefore no conversion issues with the basic integer, floating-point and string types.

All languages deal with all data types in the same way. There is also a mechanism for defining and managing new types.

4. tool Support:-

The CLR works hand-in-hand with tools like visual studio, compilers, debuggers, and profilers to make the developer's job much simpler.

5. Security:-

The CLR manages system security through user and code identity coupled with permission checks. The identity of the code can be known and permission for the use of resources granted accordingly. This type of security is a major feature of .NET. The .NET framework also provides support for role-based security using windows NT accounts and groups.

6. Automatic Resource Management:-

The .NET CLR provides efficient and automatic resource management such as memory, screen space, network connections, database, etc. CLR invokes various built-in functions of .NET framework to allocate and de-allocate the memory of .NET objects.

Therefore, programmers need not write the code to explicitly allocate and de-allocate memory to the program.

7. Easy and rich debugging support:-

The .NET IDE (integrated development environment) provides an easy and rich debugging support. Once an exception occurs at run time, the program stops and the IDE marks the line which contains the error along with the details of that error and possible solutions. The runtime also provides built-in stack walking facilities making it much easier to locate bugs and error.

8. Simplified development:-

With .NET installing or uninstalling, a window-based application is a matter of copying or deleting files. This possible because .NET components are not referenced in the registry.

9. Framework class library:-

The framework class library (FCL) of the .NET framework contains a rich collection of classes that are available for developers to use these classes in code Microsoft has developed these classes to fulfill various tasks of applications, such as working with files and other data storages, performing input-output operations, web services, data access, and drawing graphics.

The classes in the FCL are logically grouped under various namespaces such as system, System.collections, system.diagnostics, system.Globalization, system.IO, system.text etc.

10. Portability:-

The application developed in the .NET environment is portable. When the source code of a program written in a CLR compliant language complies, it generates a machine-independent and intermediate code. This was originally called the Microsoft Intermediate Language (MSIL) and has now been renamed as the common Intermediate Language (CIL). CIL is the key to portability in .NET.

•

Explain CLR Execution.

The Common Language Runtime (CLR) is programming that manages the execution of programs written in any of several supported languages, allowing them to share common object-oriented classes written in any of the languages. It is a part of Microsoft's .NET Framework. The CLR is somewhat comparable to the Java virtual machine that Sun Microsystems provides for running programs compiled from the Java language. Microsoft refers to its CLR as a "managed execution environment." A program compiled for the CLR does not need a language-specific execution environment and can easily be moved to and run on any system with Windows 2000 or Windows XP.

CLR transforms source code into a form of bytecode known as Common Intermediate Language (CIL). At run time, CLR handles the execution of the CIL code.

Following are the functions of the CLR.

- It converts the program into native code.
- Handles Exceptions
- Provides type-safety
- Memory management
- Provides security
- Improved performance
- Language independent
- Platform independent
- Garbage collection
- Provides language features such as inheritance, interfaces, and overloading for object-oriented programmings.

Components in CLR

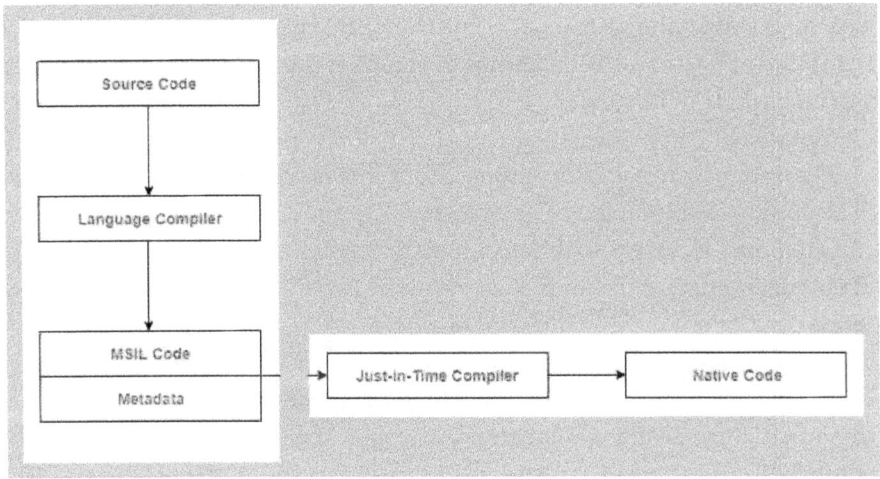

CLR using .Net Framework Class Library

Source Code:

Source code is the fundamental component of a computer program that is created by a programmer. It can be read and easily understood by a human being. When a programmer types a sequence of C programming language statements into Windows Notepad, for example, and saves the sequence as a text file, the text file is said to contain the source code.

Source code and object code are sometimes referred to as the "before" and "after" versions of a compiled computer program.

Language Compiler:

It transforms source code written in one programming language into another programming language. ... When you run the C# compiler, it takes your code as an input, does some processing, and then outputs your program in intermediate language (IL) code which is saved in *.exe or *. dll files.

MSIL Code:

Instructions that are platform independent and are generated by the language-specific compiler from the source code. The MSIL is platform independent and consequently, it can be executed on any of the Common Language Infrastructure supported environments such as the Windows *.NET* runtime.

The MSIL is converted into a particular computer environment specific machine code by the JIT compiler. This is done before the MSIL can be executed. Also, the MSIL is converted into the machine code on a requirement basis i.e. the JIT compiler compiles the MSIL as required rather than the whole of it.

Metadata

The data providing information about one or more aspects of the data; it is used to summarize basic information about data which can make tracking and working with specific data easier. Some examples include: Means of creation of the data. Purpose of the data. Time and date of creation.

Native Code

Programming code that is configured to run on a specific processor. Native code will generally not function if used on a processor other than the one it was specifically written for unless it is allowed to run over an emulator.

Common Language Specification (CLS): It is responsible for converting the different .NET programming language syntactical rules and regulations into CLR understandable format. Basically, it provides the Language Interoperability. Language Interoperability means to provide the execution support to other programming languages also in .NET framework.

Language Interoperability can be achieved in two ways :

1. **Managed Code:** The MSIL code which is managed by the CLR is known as the Managed Code. For managed code CLR provides **three** .NET facilities:
2. **Unmanaged Code:** Before .NET development the programming language like .COM Components & Win32 API do not generate the MSIL code. So these are not managed by CLR rather managed by Operating System.

Common Type System (CTS): Every programming language has its own data type system, so CTS is responsible for understanding all the data type systems of .NET programming languages and converting them into CLR understandable format which will be a common format.

There are 2 Types of CTS that every .NET programming language have :

1. **Value Types:** Value Types will store the value directly into the memory location. These types work with stack mechanism only. CLR allows memory for these at Compile Time.
2. **Reference Types:** Reference Types will contain a memory address of value because the reference types won't store the variable value directly in memory. These types work with Heap mechanism. CLR allots memory for these at Runtime.

Garbage Collector: It is used to provide the *Automatic Memory Management* feature. If there was no garbage collector, programmers would have to write the memory management codes which will be a kind of overhead on programmers.

JIT (Just In Time Compiler): It is responsible for converting the CIL(Common Intermediate Language) into machine code or native code using the Common Language Runtime environment.

Features of CLR:

1. .NET Framework Class Library support: Contains built-in types and libraries to manage assemblies, memory, security, threading, and other runtime system support
2. Debugging: Facilities for making it easier to debug code.
3. Exception management: Allows you to write code to create and handle exceptions.
4. Execution management: Manages the execution of code
5. Garbage collection: Automatic memory management and garbage collection

6. Interop: Backward-compatibility with COM and Win32 code.
7. Just-In-Time (JIT) compilation: An efficiency feature for ensuring that the CLR only compiles code just before it executes
8. Security: Traditional role-based security support, in addition to Code Access Security (CAS)
9. Thread management: Allows you to run multiple threads of execution
10. Type loading: Finds and loads assemblies and types
11. Type safety: Ensures references match compatible types, which is very useful for reliable and secure code.

Benefits of CLR:

- It improves the performance by providing a rich interact between programs at run time.
- Enhance portability by removing the need of recompiling a program on any operating system that supports it.
- Security also increases as it analyzes the MSIL instructions whether they are safe or unsafe. Also, the use of delegates in place of function pointers enhance the type safety and security.
- Support automatic memory management with the help of Garbage Collector.
- Provides cross-language integration because CTS inside CLR provides a common standard that activates the different languages to extend and share each other's libraries.
- Provides support to use the components that developed in other .NET programming languages.
- Provide language, platform, and architecture independence.
- It allows easy creation of scalable and multithreaded applications, as the developer has no need to think about the memory management and security issues.

Give the difference between OOP, POP, Event Driven programming.

Procedure Oriented	Object Oriented	Event Driven Programming
In pop, a program is divided into small parts, it is called functions.	In oop, the program is divided into small parts it is called the objects.	In Event driven action being executed is known as event driven.
Pop follows Top- down approach.	Oop follows a bottom- up approach.	Importance is given to tasks to be performed.
Pop does not have a facility to hide data. So it is less secure.	Oop has the facility to hide data, so it is more secure.	Event driven also provides data hiding. So it's more secure.
Does not have an access specifier.	Have access specifiers.	It has access specifications like private, public, protected.
To add new data and function in POP is not so easy.	To add new data and function in OOP is easy.	Easily add new data & functions.
E.g - C	E.g – C++	E.g. VB.NET, C#

Difference between POP , OOP & EDP

•

Explain C# IDE layout.

Visual Studio is the Integrated Development Environment in which developers work when creating programs in one of many languages, including C#, for the .NET Framework . It is used to create console and graphical user interface (GUI) applications along with Windows Forms or WPF (Windows Presentation Foundation) applications, web applications, and web services in both native code together with managed code for all platforms supported by Microsoft Windows, Windows Mobile, Windows CE, .NET Framework, .NET Compact Framework and Microsoft Silverlight.

C# is designed for building a variety of applications that run on the .NET Framework. Before you start learning more about C# programming, it is important to understand the development environment and identify some of the frequently using programming tools in the Visual Studio IDE.

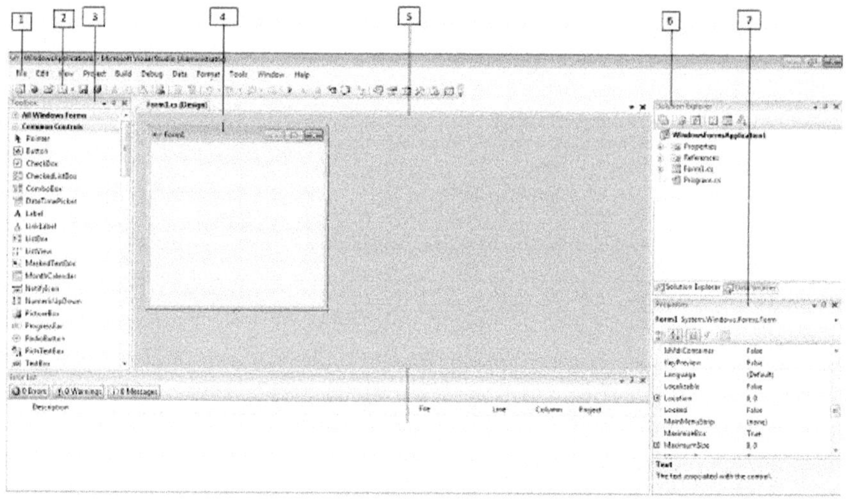

IDE Layout

- 1. Menu Bar
- 2. Standard Toolbar
- 3. ToolBox
- 4. Forms Designer
- 5. Output Window
- 6. Solution Explorer
- 7. Properties Window

Combined with the .NET Framework, C# enables the creation of Windows applications, Web services, database tools, components, controls, and more. Visual Studio organizes your work in projects and solutions. A solution can contain more than one project, such as a DLL and an executable that references that DLL. From the following C# chapters you will learn how to use these Visual Studio features for your C# programming needs.

- **Define: Namespace and write down the namespace classes.**

In C#, namespaces are used to logically arrange classes, structs, interfaces, enums and delegates. The namespaces in C# can be nested. That means one namespace can contain other namespaces also. The .NET framework already contains number of standard namespaces like System, System.Net, System.IO etc. In addition to these standard namespaces the user can define their own namespaces.

Declaring a Namespace

The C# language provide a keyword namespace to create a user defined name space. The general form of declaring a namespace is as follows.

```
namespace <namespace_name>
{
// Classes and/or structs and/or enums etc.
}
```

Example of Namespace:

```
using System;
namespace ConsoleApplication1
{
class Program
{
static void Main(string[] args)
{
Console.WriteLine("Hello Namespace!");
}
}
}
```

Example of namespace classes is given below:

```
using System;
namespace First
{
public class Hello
{
public void sayHello()
{
Console.WriteLine("Hello First Namespace");
}}}
namespace Second
```

```
{
public class Hello
{
public void sayHello()
{
Console.WriteLine("Hello Second Namespace");
}}}
public class TestNamespace
{
public static void Main()
{
First.Hello h1 = new First.Hello();
Second.Hello h2 = new Second.Hello();
h1.sayHello();
h2.sayHello();
}
}
```

In above example of namespace in C# where one namespace program accesses another namespace program. In main function we called two namespace by making their objects. When we run this program the following output will come.

Hello First Namespace
Hello Second Namespace

Define Datatype and its types

A data type specifies the type of data that a variable can store such as integer, floating, character etc.

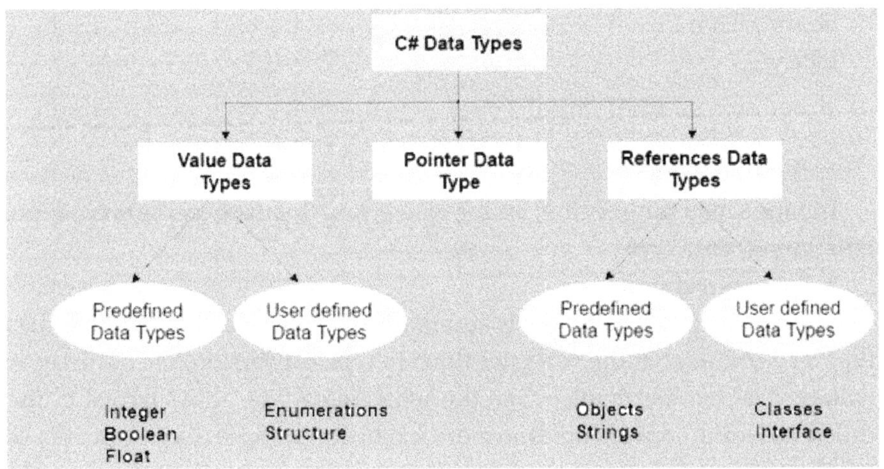

C# Data Types

There are 3 types of data types in C# language

Types: Data types:

1. Value Type Short,int,char,float,double etc.
2. Reference Type string,class,object and interface
3. Pointer Type Pointers

Explain Type Casting / Type Conversion

1. Type Casting:

In typing casting, a data type is converted into another data type by the programmer using the casting operator during the program design. In typing casting, the destination data type may be smaller than the source data type when converting the data type to another data type, that's why it is also called narrowing conversion.

Syntax/Declaration:-

destination_datatype = (target_datatype)variable;

casting operator **():**

target_datatype: is a data type in which we want to convert the source data type.

Type Casting example –

```
float x;//Line 1
byte y;
...
...
y=(byte)x; //Line 5
```

In Line 5: you can see that, we are converting **float(source) data type** into **byte(target) data type.**

2. Type conversion :

In type conversion, a data type is automatically converted into another data type by a compiler at the compiler time. In type conversion, the destination data type cannot be smaller than the source data type, that's why it is also called widening conversion. One more important thing is that it can only be applied to compatible data types.

Type Conversion example –

```
int x=30;
float y;
y=x; // y==30.000000.
```

Difference between Type casting and Type conversion

TYPE CASTING

1. In type casting, a data type is converted into another data type by a programmer using casting operator
2. Type casting can be applied to **compatible data types** as well as **incompatible data types.**
3. In type casting, casting operator is needed in order to cast the a data type to another data type.
4. In typing casting, the destination data type may be smaller than the source data type, when converting the data type to another data type.
5. Type casting takes place during the program design by programmer.
6. Type casting is also called narrowing conversion because in this, the destination data type may be smaller than the source data type.

7. Type casting is often used in coding and competitive programming works.
8. Type casting is more efficient and reliable.

TYPE CONVERSION

1. Type conversion, a data type is converted into another data type by a compiler.
2. Type conversion can only be applied to **compatible datatypes**.
3. Type conversion, there is no need for a casting operator.
4. Type conversion, the destination data type can't be smaller than source data type.
5. Type conversion is done at the compile time.
6. Type conversion is also called widening conversion because in this, the destination data type can not be smaller than the source data type.
7. Type conversion is less used in coding and competitive programming as it might cause incorrect answer.
8. Type conversion is less efficient and less reliable.

Explain Boxing and Un-Boxing with example.

Boxing and unboxing is an important concept in C#. C# Type System contains three data types: Value Types (int, char, etc), Reference Types (object) and Pointer Types. Basically, it converts a Value Type to a Reference Type, and vice versa. Boxing and Unboxing enables a unified view of the type system in which a value of any type can be treated as an object.

Boxing:

It convert value type into an object type.

Boxing is an implicit conversion process.

Here, the value stored on the stack copied to the object stored on the heap memory.

Example:

// C# program to illustrate Boxing

```
using System
public class My
{
static public void Main()
{
int val = 2019;
// Boxing
object o = val;
// Change the value of val
val = 2000;
Console.WriteLine("Value type of val is {0}", val);
Console.WriteLine("Object type of val is {0}", o);
}
}
```

Following is the output of above program:

Output:

Value type of val is 2000
Object type of val is 2019

Un - Boxing:

It convert an object type into value type.

Unboxing is the explicit conversion process.

Here, the object stored on the heap memory copied to the value stored on the stack .

Example:

```
// C# program to illustrate Unboxing
using System;
public class My {
static public void Main()
{
int val = 2019;
// Boxing
object o = val;
// Unboxing
int x = (int)o;
Console.WriteLine("Value of o is {0}", o);
Console.WriteLine("Value of x is {0}", x);
```

```
}
}
```

Following is the output of above program:

Output:

Value of o is 2019

Value of x is 2019

Explain Types of Operator

An operator is a symbol that tells the compiler to perform specific mathematical or logical manipulations. C# has rich set of built-in operators and provides the following type of operators –

- Arithmetic Operators
- Relational Operators
- Logical Operators
- Bitwise Operators
- Assignment Operators
- Misc Operators

This tutorial explains the arithmetic, relational, logical, bitwise, assignment, and other operators one by one.

Arithmetic Operators

Following table shows all the arithmetic operators supported by C#. Assume variable **A** holds 10 and variable **B** holds 20 then –+

- *+ Adds two operands* ***Example:-*** *A + B = 30*

- *- Subtracts second operand from the first* ***Example:-*** *A - B = -10*

- ** Multiplies both operands* ***Example:-*** *A * B = 200*

- *% Modulus Operator and remainder of after* **Example:-** *B % A = 0*

an integer division

- *++ Increment operator increases integer value* **Example:-** *A++ = 11*

by one

- *-- Decrement operator decreases integer value* **Example:-***A-- = 9*

by one.

Relational Operators

Following table shows all the relational operators supported by C#. Assume variable **A** holds 10 and variable **B** holds 20, then –

Operator	Description	Example
==	Checks if the values of two operands are equal or not, if yes then condition becomes true.	(A == B) is not true.
!=	Checks if the values of two operands are equal or not, if values are not equal then condition becomes true.	(A != B) is true.
>	Checks if the value of left operand is greater than the value of right operand, if yes then condition becomes true.	(A > B) is not true.
<	Checks if the value of left operand is less than the value of right operand, if yes then condition becomes true.	(A < B) is true.
>=	Checks if the value of left operand is greater than or equal to the value of right operand, if yes then condition becomes true.	(A >= B) is not true.
<=	Checks if the value of left operand is less than or equal to the value of right operand, if yes then condition becomes true.	(A <= B) is true.

Relational Operator

Logical Operators

Following table shows all the logical operators supported by C#. Assume variable **A** holds Boolean value true and variable **B** holds Boolean value false, then –

Operator	Description	Example
&&	Called Logical AND operator. If both the operands are non zero then condition becomes true.	(A && B) is false.
||	Called Logical OR Operator. If any of the two operands is non zero then condition becomes true.	(A || B) is true.
!	Called Logical NOT Operator. Use to reverses the logical state of its operand. If a condition is true then Logical NOT operator will make false.	!(A && B) is true.

Logical Operator

Bitwise Operators

Bitwise operator works on bits and perform bit by bit operation. The truth tables for &, |, and ^ are as follows –

p	q	p & q	p | q	p ^ q
0	0	0	0	0
0	1	0	1	1
1	1	1	1	0
1	0	0	1	1

Truth Table

Assume if A = 60; and B = 13; then in the binary format they are as follows –

A = 0011 1100
B = 0000 1101

A&B = 0000 1100

A|B = 0011 1101

A^B = 0011 0001

~A = 1100 0011

The Bitwise operators supported by C# are listed in the following table. Assume variable A holds 60 and variable B holds 13, then –

<table>
<tr><th>Operator</th><th>Description</th><th>Example</th></tr>
<tr><td>&</td><td>Binary AND Operator copies a bit to the result if it exists in both operands.</td><td>(A & B) = 12, which is 0000 1100</td></tr>
<tr><td>|</td><td>Binary OR Operator copies a bit if it exists in either operand.</td><td>(A | B) = 61, which is 0011 1101</td></tr>
<tr><td>^</td><td>Binary XOR Operator copies the bit if it is set in one operand but not both.</td><td>(A ^ B) = 49, which is 0011 0001</td></tr>
<tr><td>~</td><td>Binary Ones Complement Operator is unary and has the effect of 'flipping' bits.</td><td>(~A) = -61, which is 1100 0011 in 2's complement due to a signed binary number.</td></tr>
<tr><td><<</td><td>Binary Left Shift Operator. The left operands value is moved left by the number of bits specified by the right operand.</td><td>A << 2 = 240, which is 1111 0000</td></tr>
<tr><td>>></td><td>Binary Right Shift Operator. The left operands value is moved right by the number of bits specified by the right operand.</td><td>A >> 2 = 15, which is</td></tr>
</table>

Bitwise Operrator

Assignment Operators

There are following assignment operators supported by C# –

Operator	Description	Example
=	Simple assignment operator, Assigns values from right side operands to left side operand	C = A + B assigns value of A + B into C
+=	Add AND assignment operator, It adds right operand to the left operand and assign the result to left operand	C += A is equivalent to C = C + A
-=	Subtract AND assignment operator, It subtracts right operand from the left operand and assign the result to left operand	C -= A is equivalent to C = C – A
*=	Multiply AND assignment operator, It multiplies right operand with the left operand and assign the result to left operand	C *= A is equivalent to C = C * A
/=	Divide AND assignment operator, It divides left operand with the right operand and assign the result to left operand	C /= A is equivalent to C = C / A
%=	Modulus AND assignment operator, It takes modulus using two operands and assign the result to left operand	C %= A is equivalent to C = C % A

<<=	Left shift AND assignment operator	C <<= 2 is same as C = C << 2
>>=	Right shift AND assignment operator	C >>= 2 is same as C = C >> 2
&=	Bitwise AND assignment operator	C &= 2 is same as C = C & 2
^=	bitwise exclusive OR and assignment operator	C ^= 2 is same as C = C ^ 2
|=	bitwise inclusive OR and assignment operator	C |= 2 is same as C = C | 2

Assignment Operator

Miscellaneous Operators

There are few other important operators including **sizeof, typeof** and **? :** supported by C#.

Operator	Description	Example
sizeof()	Returns the size of a data type.	sizeof(int), returns 4.
typeof()	Returns the type of a class.	typeof(StreamReader);
&	Returns the address of an variable.	&a; returns actual address of the variable.
*	Pointer to a variable.	*a; creates pointer named 'a' to a variable.
? :	Conditional Expression	If Condition is true ? Then value X : Otherwise value Y
is	Determines whether an object is of a certain type.	If(Ford is Car) // checks if Ford is an object of the Car class.
as	Cast without raising an exception if the cast fails.	Object obj = new StringReader("Hello"); StringReader r = obj as StringReader;

Miscellaneous Operators

Explain Types of conditional structure.

The conditional statement requires the programmer to specify one or more conditions to be evaluated or tested by the program, along with a statement or statements to be executed if the condition is determined to be true, and optionally, other statements to be executed if the condition is determined to be false.

Sr.No	Statement & Description
1	**if statement** An if statement consists of a boolean expression followed by one or more statements.
2	**if...else statement** An if statement can be followed by an optional else statement, which executes when the boolean expression is false.
3	**nested if statements** You can use one if or else if statement inside another if or else ifstatement(s).
4	**switch statement** A switch statement allows a variable to be tested for equality against a list of values.
5	**nested switch statements** You can use one switch statement inside another switchstatement(s).

Conditional Statements

Explain WHILE loop with example.

C# While Loop

The while loop loops through a block of code as long as a specified condition is True:

Syntax

```
while (condition)
{
// code block to be executed
}
```

Example

```
int i = 0;
while (i < 10)
{
Console.WriteLine(i);
Console.ReadLine();
```

```
i++;
}
```

Explain FOR loop with example.

Following is the syntax of defining for loop in c# programming language.

Synatax:

```
for (initialization; condition; iterator(inc / dec))
{
// Statements to Execute
}
```

If you observe the above syntax, we defined a for loop with 3 parts: initialization, **condition**, **iterator**, and these are separated with a **semicolon** (;).

1. In the **initialization** part, the variable will be declared and initialized. The **initialization** part will be executed only once at the starting of the **for** loop.
2. After completion of the **initialization** part, the **condition** part will be evaluated. Here the condition is a boolean expression, and it will return either **true** or **false**.
3. In case if the **condition** is evaluated to **true**:
    - The statements inside of **for** loop will be executed.
    - After that, the **iterator** part will be executed, and it will increase or decrease the initialized variable value based on our requirements.
    - After changing the variable value, again, the **condition** will be evaluated, and execute the statements within the loop.
    - This process will continue until the **condition** is evaluated as **false**.
4. If the **condition** is evaluated to **false**, then the **for** loop execution will be stopped, and control will come out of the loop.

For example, if we have a **for loop** to print the variable (**i**) value to **4** times, the process flow of for loop will be like as shown below.

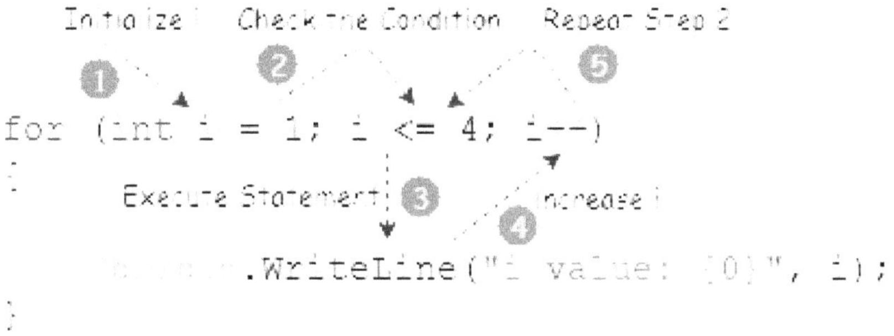

Initialize i   Check the Condition   Repeat Step 2

```
for (int i = 1; i <= 4; i--)
{
        .WriteLine("i value: {0}", i);
}
```

Execute Statement   Increase i

Working of For Loop

As discussed, first we declared and assigned a value (**1**) to the variable **i**, then the condition (**i <= 4**) will be evaluated. Since the condition is **true**, then the statements within the loop will be executed.

After that, the iterator (**i++**) will be evaluated, and it will increase the value of a variable (**i**). Again the condition (**i <= 4**) checking will happen, and it will continue until the condition returns **true**.

Here the condition will return **true** till the variable **i** value becomes **4. After** that, if **i** value becomes **5**, then the condition (**5 <= 4**) will fail, and it returns **false**.

C# For Loop Flowchart Diagram

Following is the pictorial representation of **for** loop process flow diagram in the c# programming language.

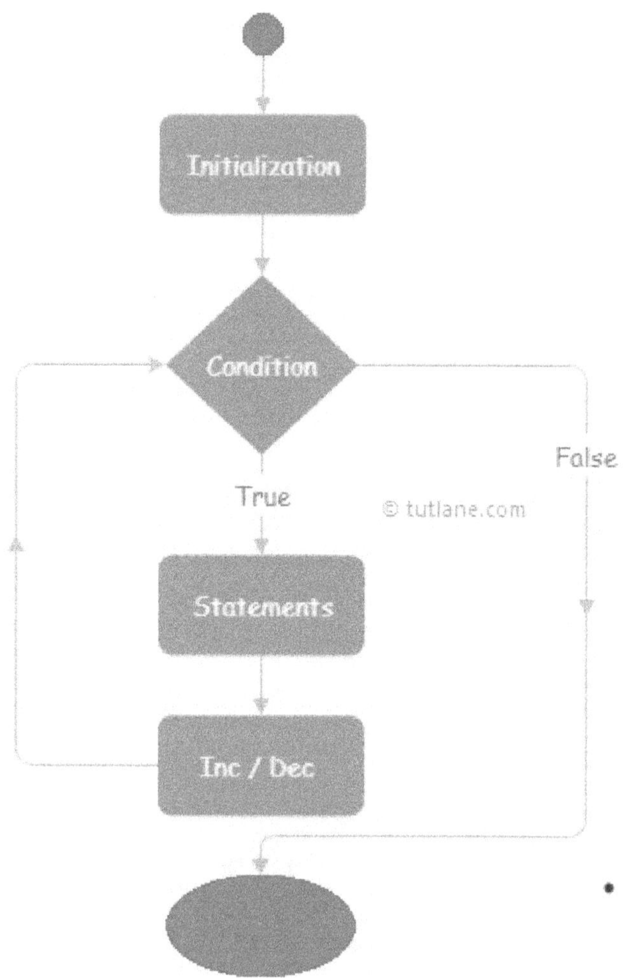

Flowchart Diagram of For Loop

Example

Following is the example of using for loop in c# programming language to iterate or loop through a particular list of statements.

```
using System;

namespace first
{
class Program
```

```
{
static void Main(string[] args)
{
for (int i = 1; i <= 4; i++)
{
Console.WriteLine("i value: {0}", i);
}
Console.WriteLine("Press Enter Key to Exit..");
Console.ReadLine();
}
}
}
```

Explain DO WHILE loop with example.

The do while loop is the same as while loop except that it executes the code block at least once.

Syntax:

```
do
{
//code block
} while(condition);
```

The do-while loop starts with the do keyword followed by a code block and a boolean expression with the while keyword. The do while loop stops execution exits when a boolean condition evaluates to false. Because the while(condition) specified at the end of the block, it certainly executes the code block at least once.

Example:

```
int i = 0;
do
{
Console.WriteLine("i = {0}", i);
i++;
} while (i < 10);
```

Explain Jagged array with example.

Jagged array is a **array of arrays** such that member arrays can be of different sizes. In other words, the length of each array index can differ. The elements of Jagged Array are reference types and initialized to null by default. Jagged Array can also be mixed with multidimensional arrays. Here, the number of rows will be fixed at the declaration time, but you can vary the number of columns.

Declaration

In Jagged arrays, user has to provide the number of rows only. If the user is also going to provide the number of columns, then this array will be no more Jagged Array.

Syntax:

```
data_type[][] name_of_array = new data_type[rows][]
```

Example:

```
int[][] jagged_arr = new int[4][]
```

In the above example, a single-dimensional array is declared that has 4 elements(rows), each of which is a 1-D array of integers.

Initialization

The elements of Jagged Array **must be initialized** before its use. You can separately initialize each array element. There are many ways to initialize the Jagged array's element.

Example 1:

Providing the size of each array elements separately. Here each of the elements is a 1-D array of integers where:

- The first row or element is an array of 2 integers.
- The second row or element is an array of 4 integers.
- The third row or element is an array of 6 integers.
- The fourth row or element is an array of 7 integers.

```
jagged_arr[0] = new int[2];
jagged_arr[1] = new int[4];
jagged_arr[2] = new int[6];
jagged_arr[3] = new int[7];
```

Example 2:

When the array size is not needed then its elements can be initialized with direct values as follows:

```
jagged_arr[0] = new int[] {1, 2, 3, 4};
jagged_arr[1] = new int[] {11, 34, 67};
```

```
jagged_arr[2] = new int[] {89, 23};
jagged_arr[3] = new int[] {0, 45, 78, 53, 99};
```

Declaration as well as Initialization

Example 1: Using the Direct Method

```
int[][] jagged_arr = new int[][]
{
new int[] {1, 2, 3, 4},
new int[] {11, 34, 67},
new int[] {89, 23},
new int[] {0, 45, 78, 53, 99}
};
```

Example 2: Using Short-hand Method. There is no default initialization for the elements so a user cannot omit the new operator from the elements initialization.

```
int[][] jagged_arr =
{
new int[] {1, 2, 3, 4},
new int[] {11, 34, 67},
new int[] {89, 23},
new int[] {0, 45, 78, 53, 99}
};
```

Accessing the Elements

To access the elements of the Jagged array user has to specify the row and column with the array name.

Example:

```
// Accessing & Assigning 99 to the third element ([2]) of the second array ([1])
jagged_arr[1][2] = 99;
// Accessing & Assigning 47 to the first element ([0]) of the fourth array ([3]):
jagged_arr[3][0] = 47;
```

Program:

```
// C# program to illustrate the declaration and Initialization of Jagged Arrays
using System;
class first {
// Main Method
public static void Main()
```

```
{
// Declare the Jagged Array of four elements:
int[][] jagged_arr = new int[4][];
// Initialize the elements
jagged_arr[0] = new int[] {1, 2, 3, 4};
jagged_arr[1] = new int[] {11, 34, 67};
jagged_arr[2] = new int[] {89, 23};
jagged_arr[3] = new int[] {0, 45, 78, 53, 99};
// Display the array elements:
for (int n = 0; n < jagged_arr.Length; n++) {
// Print the row number
System.Console.Write("Row({0}): ", n);
for (int k = 0; k < jagged_arr[n].Length; k++) {
// Print the elements in the row
System.Console.Write("{0} ", jagged_arr[n][k]);
}
System.Console.WriteLine();
}
}
}
```

Following is the Output:

```
Row(0): 1 2 3 4
Row(1): 11 34 67
Row(2): 89 23
Row(3): 0 45 78 53 99
```

Explain param parameters with example.

```
using System;
namespace ArrayDemo
{
class ParamArray
{
public int AddElements(params int[] arr)
{
int sum = 0;
foreach (int i in arr)
{
```

```
sum += i;
}
return sum;
}
}
class FirstClass {
static void Main(string[] args) {
ParamArray app = new ParamArray();
int sum = app.AddElements(512, 720, 250, 567, 889);
Console.WriteLine("The sum is: {0}", sum);
Console.ReadKey();
}
}
}
```

Following is the Output:

The sum is: 2938

Explain REF and OUT keywords with example.

The **out** is a keyword in C# which is used for the passing the arguments to methods as a reference type. It is generally used when a method returns multiple values. The out parameter does not pass the property.

Example :

```
// C# program to illustrate the concept of out parameter
using System;
class first {
// Main method
static public void Main()
{
// Declaring variable
// without assigning value
int G;
// Pass variable G to the method
// using out keyword
Sum(out G);
// Display the value G
Console.WriteLine("The sum of" + " the value is: {0}", G);
}
```

```
// Method in which out parameter is passed and this method returns the value of the passed parameter
public static void Sum(out int G)
{
G = 80;
G += G;
}
}
```

Output:

The sum of the value is: 160

The **ref** is a keyword in C# which is used for the passing the arguments by a reference. Or we can say that if any changes made in this argument in the method will reflect in that variable when the control return to the calling method. The *ref* parameter does not pass the property.

Example:

```
// C# program to illustrate the concept of ref parameter
using System;
class first {
// Main Method
public static void Main()
{
// Assign string value
string str = "Kinnari";
// Pass as a reference parameter
SetValue(ref str);
// Display the given string
Console.WriteLine(str);
}
static void SetValue(ref string str1)
{
// Check parameter value
if (str1 == "Kinnari") {
Console.WriteLine("Hello!!Kinnari");
}
// Assign the new value
// of the parameter
str1 = "KinnariMishra";
}
```

}

Difference between ref and out keyword.

ref keyword

1. It is necessary the parameters should initialize before it pass to ref.
2. It is not necessary to initialize the value of a parameter before returning to the calling method.
3. The passing of value through ref parameter is useful when the called method also need to change the value of passed parameter.
4. When ref keyword is used the data may pass in bi-directional.

out keyword

1. It is not necessary to initialize parameters before it pass to out.
2. It is necessary to initialize the value of a parameter before returning to the calling method.
3. The declaring of parameter through out parameter is useful when a method return multiple values.
4. When out keyword is used the data only passed in unidirectional.

Explain method Overloading with example.

Method Overloading is the common way of implementing polymorphism. It is the ability to redefine a function in more than one form. A user can implement function overloading by defining two or more functions in a class sharing the same name. C# can distinguish the methods with **different method signatures**. i.e. the methods can have the same name but with different parameters list (i.e. the number of the parameters, order of the parameters, and data types of the parameters) within the same class.

- Overloaded methods are differentiated based on the number and type of the parameters passed as arguments to the methods.

- You can not define more than one method with the same name, Order and the type of the arguments. It would be compiler error.
- The compiler does not consider the return type while differentiating the overloaded method. But you cannot declare two methods with the same signature and different return type. It will throw a compile-time error. If both methods have the same parameter types, but different return type, then it is not possible.

Why do we need Method Overloading?

If we need to do the same kind of the operation in different ways i.e. for different inputs. In the example described below, we are doing the addition operation for different inputs. It is hard to find many different meaningful names for single action.

Different ways of doing overloading methods-

Method overloading can be done by changing:

1. The number of parameters in two methods.
2. The data types of the parameters of methods.
3. The Order of the parameters of methods.

By changing the Number of Parameters

// C# program to demonstrate the function overloading by changing the Number of parameters

```
using System;
class first {
// adding two integer values.
public int Add(int a, int b)
{
int sum = a + b;
return sum;
}
// adding three integer values.
public int Add(int a, int b, int c)
{
int sum = a + b + c;
return sum;
}
// Main Method
```

```
public static void Main(String[] args)
{
// Creating Object
first ob = new first();
int sum1 = ob.Add(1, 2);
Console.WriteLine("sum of the two " + "integer value : " + sum1);
int sum2 = ob.Add(1, 2, 3);
Console.WriteLine("sum of the three "+ "integer value : " + sum2);
}
}
```

Output:

sum of the two integer value : 3
sum of the three integer value : 6

Explain Access Modifier

Access Modifiers are keywords that define the accessibility of a member, class or datatype in a program. These are mainly used to restrict unwanted data manipulation by external programs or classes. There are **4** access modifiers (public, protected, internal, private) which defines the **6 accessibility levels** as follows:

The Accessibility table of these modifiers is given below:

|	public	Protected	internal	protected internal	private	private protected
Entire program	Yes	No	No	No	No	No
Containing class	Yes	Yes	Yes	Yes	Yes	Yes
Current assembly	Yes	No	Yes	Yes	No	No
Derived types	Yes	Yes	No	Yes	No	No
Derived types within current assembly	Yes	Yes	Yes	Yes	No	Yes

Accessibility of Access Modifier

public Accessibility Level

Access is granted to the entire program. This means that another method or another assembly which contains the class reference can access these members or types. This access modifier has the most permissive access level in comparison to all other access modifiers.

Syntax:

public TypeName

Example: Here, we declare a class *Student* which consists of two class members *rollNo* and *name* which are public. These members can access from anywhere throughout the code in the current and another assembly in the program. The methods *getRollNo* and *getName* are also declared as public.

```
// C# Program to show the use of
// public Access Modifier
usingSystem;
namespacepublicAccessModifier {
classStudent {
```

```
// Declaring members rollNo
// and name as public
publicintrollNo;
publicstringname;
// Constructor
publicStudent(intr, stringn)
{
rollNo = r;
name = n;
}
// methods getRollNo and getName
// also declared as public
publicintgetRollNo()
{
returnrollNo;
}
publicstringgetName()
{
returnname;
}
}
classProgram {
// Main Method
staticvoidMain(string[] args)
{
// Creating object of the class Student
Student S = newStudent(1, "Vidya");
// Displaying details directly
// using the class members
// accessible through another method
Console.WriteLine("Roll number: {0}", S.rollNo);
Console.WriteLine("Name: {0}", S.name);
Console.WriteLine();
// Displaying details using
// member method also public
Console.WriteLine("Roll number: {0}", S.getRollNo());
Console.WriteLine("Name: {0}", S.getName());
}
```

```
}
}
```

Output:

Roll number: 1
Name: Vidya
Roll number: 1
Name: Vidya

Explain MESSAGE BOX with its Syntax and example.

A message box or dialog box is used to interact with the users of your application. The purpose of using a message box may include notifying about a particular action e.g. success message after entering a record. Similarly, an error message if an operation was unsuccessful. In both cases, you may display the "OK" button in the message box with the message.

A MessageBox can have different button combinations such as YesNo and OKCancel. The MessageBoxButtons enumeration represents the buttons to be displayed on a MessageBox and has following values.

- OK
- OKCancel
- AbortRetryIgnore
- YesNoCancel
- YesNo
- RetryCancel

The following code snippet creates a MessageBox with a title and Yes and No buttons. This is a typical MessageBox you may call when you want to close an application. If the Yes button is clicked, the application will be closed. The Show method returns a DialogResult enumeration.

```
string message = "Do you want to close this window?";
string title = "Close Window";
MessageBoxButtons buttons = MessageBoxButtons.YesNo;
DialogResult result = MessageBox.Show(message, title, buttons);
if (result == DialogResult.Yes) {
this.Close();
} else {
// Do something
```

Explain INPUT BOX with its Syntax and example.

Follow Below steps to create InputBox.

1. Right Click on Project
2. Add References
3. Microsoft VisualBasic
4. Add namespace -> using Microsoft.VisualBasic;

Example:

```
using Microsoft.VisualBasic;
private void Form1_Load(object sender, EventArgs e)
{
int a, b, c;
a = int.Parse(Interaction.InputBox("Input First value", "Enter first value", "Enter Interger Value", -1, -1));
b = int.Parse(Interaction.InputBox("Input Second value", "Enter second value", "Enter Interger Value", -1, -1));
c = a + b;
MessageBox.Show(c.ToString(),"Addition of 2 values",MessageBoxButtons.OKCancel,MessageBoxIcon.Information);
}
```

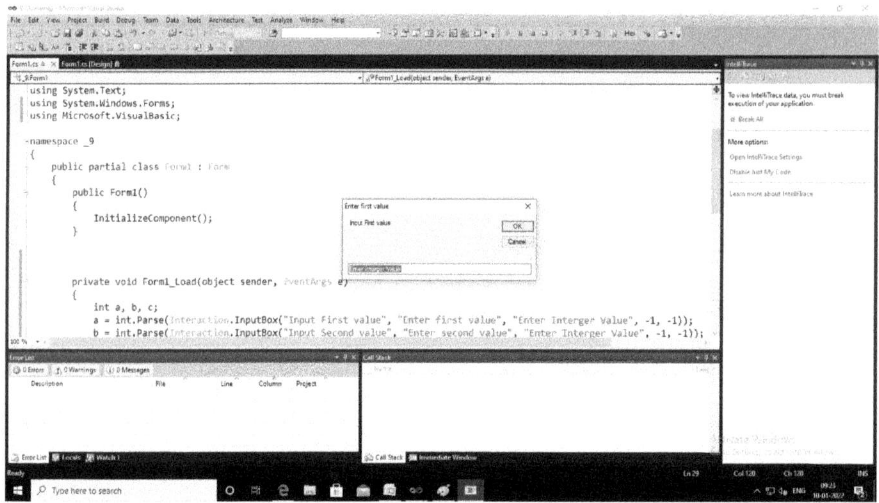

InputBox Example

Explain Font Dialog box with example.

Coding for Button Click Event

You can add a button click event handler by simply double clicking on the buttoon control. On this button control event handler, we can change the font of the text displayed in label.

```
public partial class Form1 : Form
{
public Form1()
{
InitializeComponent();
}
privatevoid button1_Click(object sender, EventArgs e)
{
DialogResult fontResult = fontDialog1.ShowDialog();
if (fontResult == DialogResult.OK)
{
label1.Font = fontDialog1.Font;
}
```

```
}
}
```

Explain Color Dialog box with example.

```
using System;
using System.Drawing;
using System.Windows.Forms;
namespace WindowsFormsApplication1
{
public partial class Form1 : Form
{
public Form1()
{
InitializeComponent();
}
private void button1_Click(object sender, EventArgs e)
{
ColorDialog dlg = new ColorDialog();
dlg.ShowDialog();
if (dlg.ShowDialog() == DialogResult.OK)
{
string str = null;
str = dlg.Color.Name;
MessageBox.Show (str);
}
}
}
}
```

Explain Open Dialog box with example.

following code snippet is the code for Browse button click event handler. Once a text file is selected, the name of the text file is displayed in the TextBox.

```
privatevoid BrowseButton_Click(object sender, EventArgs e)
{
OpenFileDialog openFileDialog1 = new OpenFileDialog
```

```
{
InitialDirectory = @"D:\",
Title = "Browse Text Files",
CheckFileExists = true,
CheckPathExists = true,
DefaultExt = "txt",
Filter = "txt files (*.txt)|*.txt",
FilterIndex = 2,
RestoreDirectory = true,
ReadOnlyChecked = true,
ShowReadOnly = true
};
if (openFileDialog1.ShowDialog() == DialogResult.OK)
{
textBox1.Text = openFileDialog1.FileName;
}
}
```

Explain Save Dialog box with example.

A SaveFileDialog control is used to save a file using Windows SaveFileDialog. A typical SaveFileDialog looks like Figure 1 where you can see the Windows Explorer type features to navigate through folders and save a file in a folder.

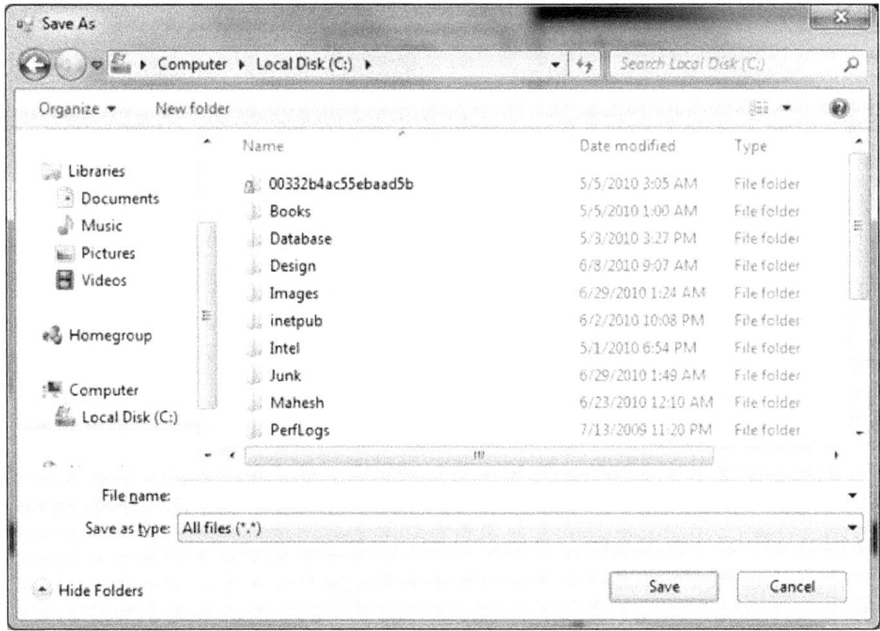

Select Location to save file

Creating a SaveFileDialog

We can create a SaveFileDialog control using a Forms designer at design-time or using the SaveFileDialog class in code at run-time (also known as dynamically). Unlike other Windows Forms controls, a SaveFileDialog does not have and not need visual properties like others.

Example:

```
privatevoid SaveButton_Click(object sender, EventArgs e) {
SaveFileDialog saveFileDialog1 = new SaveFileDialog();
saveFileDialog1.InitialDirectory = @ "C:\";
saveFileDialog1.Title = "Save text Files";
saveFileDialog1.CheckFileExists = true;
saveFileDialog1.CheckPathExists = true;
saveFileDialog1.DefaultExt = "txt";
saveFileDialog1.Filter = "Text files (*.txt)|*.txt|All files (*.*)|*.*";
saveFileDialog1.FilterIndex = 2;
saveFileDialog1.RestoreDirectory = true;
if (saveFileDialog1.ShowDialog() == DialogResult.OK) {
```

```
textBox1.Text = saveFileDialog1.FileName;
}
}
```

Explain Print Dialog box with example.

A PrintDialog control is used to open the Windows Print Dialog and let the user select the printer, set printer and paper properties, and print a file. A typical Open File Dialog looks like Figure 1 where you select a printer from available printers, set printer properties, set print range, number of pages and copies and so on. Clicking on the OK button sends the document to the printer.

Run-time

Creating a PrintDialog control at run-time is simple. The first step is to create an instance of PrintDialog class and then call the ShowDialog method. The following code snippet creates a PrintDialog control.

```
PrintDialog PrintDialog1 = newPrintDialog();
PrintDialog1.ShowDialog();
```

Printing Documents

PrintDocument object represents a document to be printed. Once a PrintDocument is created, we can set the Document property of PrintDialog as this document. After that we can also set other properties.The following code snippet creates a PrintDialog and sends some text to a printer.

```
privatevoid PrintButton_Click(object sender, EventArgs e) {
PrintDialog printDlg = newPrintDialog();
PrintDocument printDoc = newPrintDocument();
printDoc.DocumentName = "Print Document";
printDlg.Document = printDoc;
printDlg.AllowSelection = true;
printDlg.AllowSomePages = true;
//Call ShowDialog
if (printDlg.ShowDialog() == DialogResult.OK) printDoc.Print();
}
```

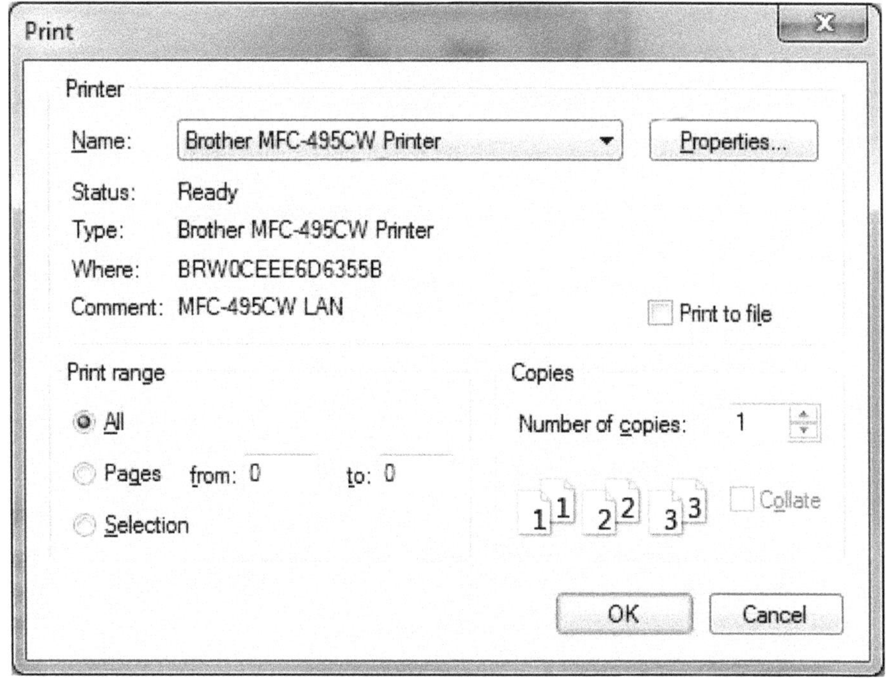

print settings

Explain Structure Exception handling with example.

An exception is defined as an event that occurs during the execution of a program that is unexpected by the program code. The actions to be performed in case of occurrence of an exception is not known to the program. In such a case, we create an exception object and call the exception handler code. The execution of an exception handler so that the program code does not crash is called exception handling. Exception handling is important because it gracefully handles an unwanted event, an exception so that the program code still makes sense to the user.

Only the structured exception handling is suppoted by the C#.Net. Unstructured exception handling is not supported by C#.

Following are the keywords of exception handling.

try:

Used to define a try block. This block holds the code that may throw an exception.

catch

Used to define a catch block. This block catches the exception thrown by the try block.

finally

Used to define the finally block. This block holds the default code.

throw

Used to throw an exception manually.

```
// C# program to show how
// Exceptions occur in a program
using System;
class first {
static void Main(string[] args)
{
// Declare an array of max index 4
int[] arr = { 1, 2, 3, 4, 5 };
// Display values of array elements
for (int i = 0; i < arr.Length; i++) {
Console.WriteLine(arr[i]);
}
// Try to access invalid index of array
Console.WriteLine(arr[7]);
// An exception is thrown upon executing
// the above line
}
}
```

Runtime Error:

Unhandled Exception:
System.IndexOutOfRangeException: Index was outside the bounds of the array.
at GFG.Main (System.String[] args) [0x0002e] in <9fa39b3b4dec49eb8af89dc70d5a0618>:0
[ERROR] FATAL UNHANDLED EXCEPTION: System.IndexOutOfRangeException: Index was outside the bounds of the array.
at first.Main (System.String[] args) [0x0002e] in <9fa39b3b4dec49eb8af89dc70d5a0618>:0

Output:

```
1
2
3
4
5
```

In the code given above, the array named 'arr' is defined for 5 elements, indices 0 to 4. When we try to access the 7th element of the array, that is non-existent, program code throws an exception and the above message is displayed. The exception can be handled using the *System.Exception* class of C#. This will be depicted in the code given below.

Exception Handling Using try-catch block

The code given below shows how we can handle exceptions using the try-catch block. The code that may generate an exception is placed inside the try block. In this case, the access to the 7th element is put inside the try block. When that statement is executed an exception is generated, which is caught by the catch block. The object of the type *IndexOutOfRangeException* is used to display a message to the user about the exception that has occurred.

Syntax:

```
try
{
// statements that may cause an exception
}
catch( Exception obj)
{
// handler code
}
```

```
// Exception handling of above code
// using try catch blocks
using System;
class Program : System.Exception {
static void Main(string[] args)
{
// Declare an array of max index 4
int[] arr = { 1, 2, 3, 4, 5 };
// Display values of array elements
for (int i = 0; i < arr.Length; i++) {
Console.WriteLine(arr[i]);
}
```

```
try {
// Try to access invalid index of array
Console.WriteLine(arr[7]);
// An exception is thrown upon executing
// the above line
}
catch (IndexOutOfRangeException e) {
// The Message property of the object
// of type IndexOutOfRangeException
// is used to display the type of exception
// that has occurred to the user.
Console.WriteLine("An Exception has occurred : {0}", e.Message);
}
}
}
```

Output:

```
1
2
3
4
5
An Exception has occurred : Index was outside the bounds of the array.
```

Using Multiple try-catch blocks

In the code given below, we attempt to generate an exception in the try block and catch it in one of the multiple catch blocks. Multiple catch blocks are used when we are not sure about the exception type that may be generated, so we write different blocks to tackle any type of exception that is encountered.

The finally block is the part of the code that has to be executed irrespective of if the exception was generated or not. In the program given below the elements of the array are displayed in the finally block.

Syntax:

```
try
{
// statements that may cause an exception
}
catch(Specific_Exception_type obj)
{
```

```
// handler code
}
catch(Specific_Exception_type obj)
{
// handler code
}
finally
{
//default code
}
// C# Program to show use of
// multiple try catch blocks
using System;
class Program {
static void Main(string[] args)
{
int[] arr = {19, 0, 75, 52};
try {
// Try to generate an exception
for (int i = 0; i < arr.Length; i++) {
Console.WriteLine(arr[i] / arr[i + 1]);
}
}
// Catch block for invalid array access
catch (IndexOutOfRangeException e) {
Console.WriteLine("An Exception has occurred : {0}", e.Message);
}
// Catch block for attempt to divide by zero
catch (DivideByZeroException e) {
Console.WriteLine("An Exception has occurred : {0}", e.Message);
}
// Catch block for value being out of range
catch (ArgumentOutOfRangeException e) {
Console.WriteLine("An Exception has occurred : {0}", e.Message);
}
// Finally block
// Will execute irrespective of the above catch blocks
finally {
```

```
for (int i = 0; i < arr.Length; i++) {
Console.Write(" {0}", arr[i]);
}
}
}
}
```

Output:

An Exception has occurred : Attempted to divide by zero.
19 75 52

Explain Exception classes

C# .NET includes built-in exception classes for every possible error. The Exception class is the base class of all the exception classes.

The following is a hierarchy of exception classes in .NET:

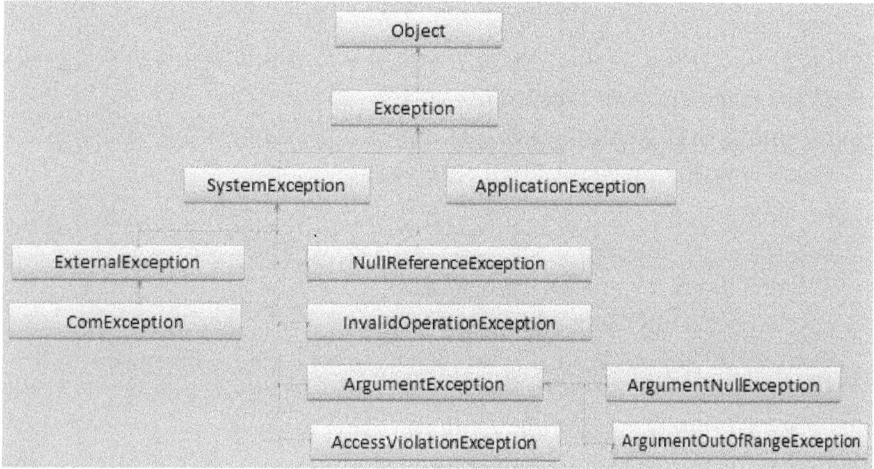

Exception Handling

Built-in Exception Classes

The following table lists important built-in exception classes in .NET.

Exception Class	Description
ArgumentException	Raised when a non-null argument that is passed to a method is invalid.
ArgumentNullException	Raised when null argument is passed to a method.
ArgumentOutOfRangeException	Raised when the value of an argument is outside the range of valid values.
DivideByZeroException	Raised when an integer value is divide by zero.
FileNotFoundException	Raised when a physical file does not exist at the specified location.
FormatException	Raised when a value is not in an appropriate format to be converted from a string by a conversion method such as Parse.
IndexOutOfRangeException	Raised when an array index is outside the lower or upper bounds of an array or collection.
InvalidOperationException	Raised when a method call is invalid in an object's current state.
KeyNotFoundException	Raised when the specified key for accessing a member in a collection is not exists.
NotSupportedException	Raised when a method or operation is not supported.
NullReferenceException	Raised when program access members of null object.
OverflowException	Raised when an arithmetic, casting, or conversion operation results in an overflow.
OutOfMemoryException	Raised when a program does not get enough memory to execute the code.
StackOverflowException	Raised when a stack in memory overflows.
TimeoutException	The time interval allotted to an operation has expired.

Exception Classes

Explain Context menu and menu strip with example.

To create a ContextMenuStrip control at design-time, you simply drag and drop a ContextMenuStrip control from Toolbox onto a Form in Visual Studio. After you drag and drop a ContextMenuStrip on a Form, the ContextMenuStrip1 is added to the FormAns:

A ToolStripMenuItem represents a menu items. The following code snippet creates a menu item at run-time and sets its properties.

```
// Create a Menu Item
ToolStripMenuItem FileMenu = new ToolStripMenuItem("File");
FileMenu.BackColor = Color.OrangeRed;
FileMenu.ForeColor = Color.Black;
FileMenu.Text = "File Menu";
FileMenu.Font = new Font("Georgia", 16);
FileMenu.TextAlign = ContentAlignment.BottomRight;
FileMenu.ToolTipText = "Click Me";
```

Explain MDI form with an example.

Ans: A Multiple Document Interface (MDI) programs can display multiple child windows inside them. This is in contrast to single document interface (SDI) applications, which can manipulate only one document at a time. Visual Studio Environment is an example of Multiple Document Interface (MDI) and notepad is an example of an SDI application. MDI applications often have a Window menu item with submenus for switching between windows or documents.

Any windows can become an MDI parent, if you set the IsMdiContainer property to True.

```
IsMdiContainer = true;
using System;
using System.Drawing;
using System.Windows.Forms;
namespace WindowsFormsApplication1
{
public partial class Form1 : Form
{
public Form1()
{
InitializeComponent();
}
private void Form1_Load(object sender, EventArgs e)
{
IsMdiContainer = true;
}
private void menu1ToolStripMenuItem_Click(object sender, EventArgs e)
{
Form2 frm2 = new Form2();
frm2.Show();
frm2.MdiParent = this;
}
private void menu2ToolStripMenuItem_Click(object sender, EventArgs e)
{
Form3 frm3 = new Form3();
frm3.Show();
```

```
frm3.MdiParent = this;
}
}
}
```

Explain ADO.Net Architecture with diagram.

ADO stands for Active Data Objects. ADO is nothing but a component in .NET Framework that helps us to fetch data from different data sources to our C# and VB.NET code and probably you can send data from your C# or VB.NET code to different data sources.

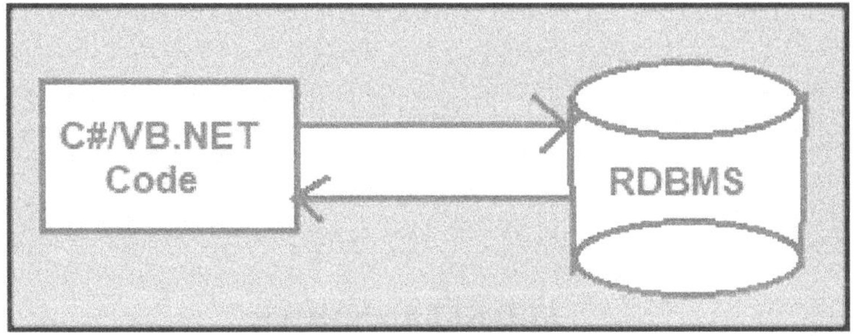

ADO.NET Diagram

The architecture of ADO.NET:

The ADO.NET Architecture is comprising of 6 important components. They are as follows:

1. **Connection**
2. **Command**
3. **DataReader**
4. **DataAdapter**
5. **DataSet**
6. **DataView**

From the above components, two components are compulsory. One is the command object and the other one is the connection object. Irrespective of the operations like Insert, Update, Delete and Select, the command and connection object you always need. For better understanding, please have a look at the following image.

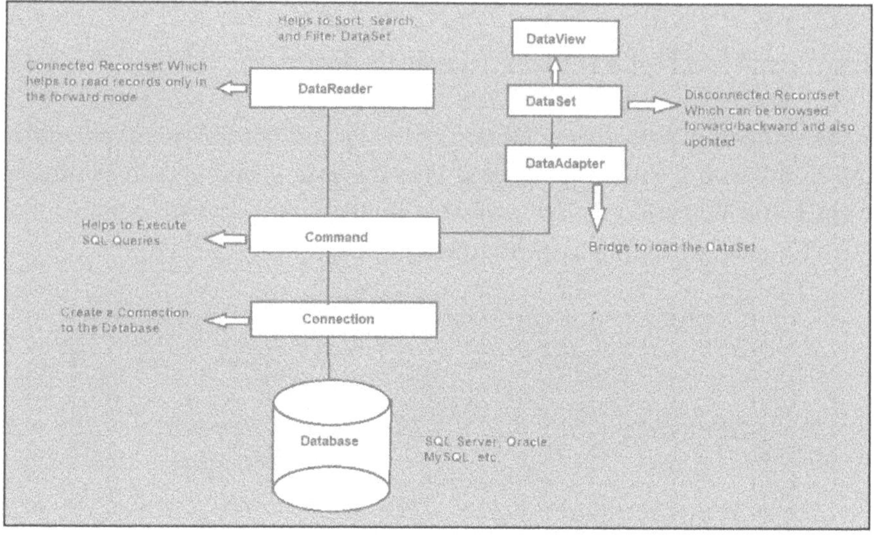

ADO.NET Architecture

Connection:

The first important component is the connection object. The connection object is required to connect with your backend database which can be SQL Server, Oracle, MySQL, etc. To create a connection object, you need at least two things. The first one is where is your database located i.e. the Machine name or IP Address or someplace where your database is located. And the second thing is the security credentials i.e. whether it is a windows authentication or user name and password-based authentication. So, the first is to create the connection object and the connection is required to connect to the backend data source.

Command:

The second important component is the command object. When we talk about databases like SQL Server, Oracle, MySQL, then understand SQL. The command object is the component where you go and write your SQL queries. Later you take the command object and execute it over the connection. Then you can fetch data or send data to the database using the command object and SQL queries.

DataReader:

DataReader is a read-only connected recordset that helps us to read the records only in the forward mode. Here, you need to understand three things i.e. read-only, connected, and forward mode.

DataSet:

It is a disconnected recordset that can be browsed in both i.e. forward and backward. It is also possible to update via dataset. DataSet gets filled by somebody called **DataAdapter.**

The DataAdapter acts as a bridge between the command object and the dataset. What the DataAdapter does, it takes the data from the command object and fills the data set.

PRACTICALS FOR PRACTICE:

PRATICAL 1:

Write a c# program to print your personal details in separate line.

```
using System;
using System.Collections.Generic;
using System.Linq;
using System.Text;
namespace practical_2
{
class Program
{
static void Main(string[] args)
{
Console.WriteLine("HELLO \nMy name is dhruvi\nI am from vadodara\nI am studing computer engineering in diploma from Parul University \nMy hobby is to play badminton\n");
}}}
```

OUTPUT:

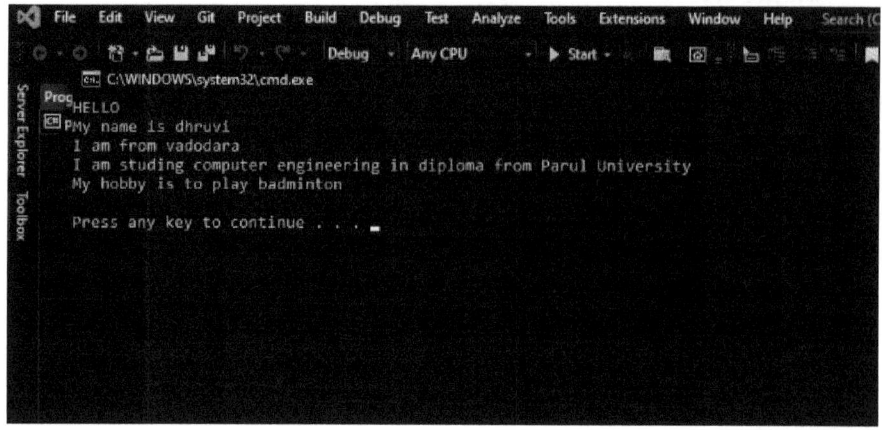

Output of Prog.1

PRACTICAL 2:

Write a c# program to print addtion of two values entered by user.

```
using System;
using System.Collections.Generic;
using System.Linq;
using System.Text;
namespace PRACTICAL_3
{
class Program
{
static void Main(string[] args)
{
int a, b, c, d;
Console.WriteLine("Enter First Value");
a = Convert.ToInt16(Console.ReadLine());
Console.WriteLine("Enter second Valuue");
b = Convert.ToInt16(Console.ReadLine());
c = a + b;
d = a / b;
Console.WriteLine("Addition is {0} and Divison is {1}", c ,d);
Console.ReadLine();
}}}
```

OUTPUT:

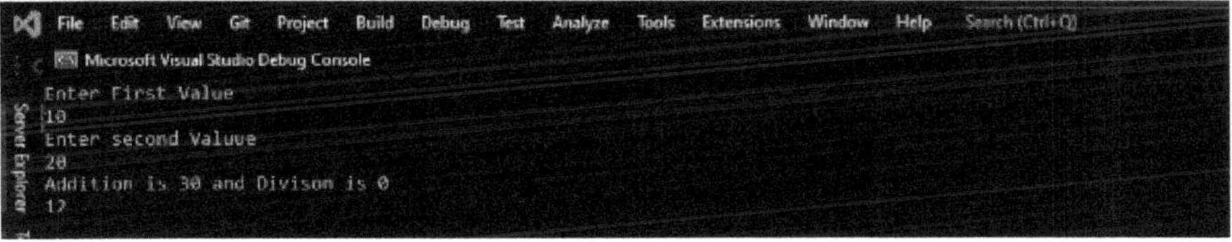

Output of Prog. 2

PRACTICAL 3:

Create windows application to make simple calculator.

```
using System;
using System.Collections.Generic;
using System.ComponentModel;
using System.Data;
using System.Drawing;
using System.Linq;
using System.Text;
using System.Windows.Forms;
namespace PRATICAL_8._1
{
public partial class Form1 : Form
{
public Form1()
{
InitializeComponent();
}
private void btnAdd_Click(object sender, EventArgs e)
{
int a, b, c;
a = Convert.ToInt16(txtFV.Text);
b = Convert.ToInt16(txtSV.Text);
c = a + b;
txtResult.Text = c.ToString();
}
private void btnSub_Click(object sender, EventArgs e)
{
```

```
int a, b, c;
a = Convert.ToInt16(txtFV.Text);
b = Convert.ToInt16(txtSV.Text);
c = a - b;
txtResult.Text = c.ToString();
}
private void btnMul_Click(object sender, EventArgs e)
{
int a, b, c;
a = Convert.ToInt16(txtFV.Text);
b = Convert.ToInt16(txtSV.Text);
c = a * b;
txtResult.Text = c.ToString();
}
private void btnDiv_Click(object sender, EventArgs e)
{
int a, b, c;
a = Convert.ToInt16(txtFV.Text);
b = Convert.ToInt16(txtSV.Text);
c = a / b;
txtResult.Text = c.ToString();
}
private void Form1_Load(object sender, EventArgs e)
{
MessageBox.Show("Me+ssage Box Example", "Example",
MessageBoxButtons.OKCancel, MessageBoxIcon.Information);
}}}
```

OUTPUT:

Enter First Value 560

Enter Second Value 89

+ - * /

Result 471

Output of Prog. 3

PRACTICAL 4:

Create windows application to make simple calculator.

```
using System;
using System.Collections.Generic;
using System.ComponentModel;
using System.Data;
using System.Drawing;
using System.Linq;
using System.Text;
using System.Windows.Forms;
namespace PRATICAL_9
{
public partial class frmRegit : Form
{
public frmRegit()
{
InitializeComponent();
} private void btnSubmit_Click(object sender, EventArgs e)
{
lstDetails.Items.Add("Your Name is: " +txtname.Text);
lstDetails.Items.Add("Your PhoneNo is: " +txtphone.Text);
lstDetails.Items.Add("Your EnrollNo is: " +txtenroll.Text);
```

```
lstDetails.Items.Add("Your City is: " +txtcity.Text);
lstDetails.Items.Add("Your Sate is: " +txtstate.Text);
lstDetails.Items.Add("Your Branch is: " +txtbranch.Text);
lstDetails.Items.Add("Your Sem is: " +txtsem.Text);
lstDetails.Items.Add("Your Address is: " +txtaddress.Text);
}
}
}
```

OUTPUT:

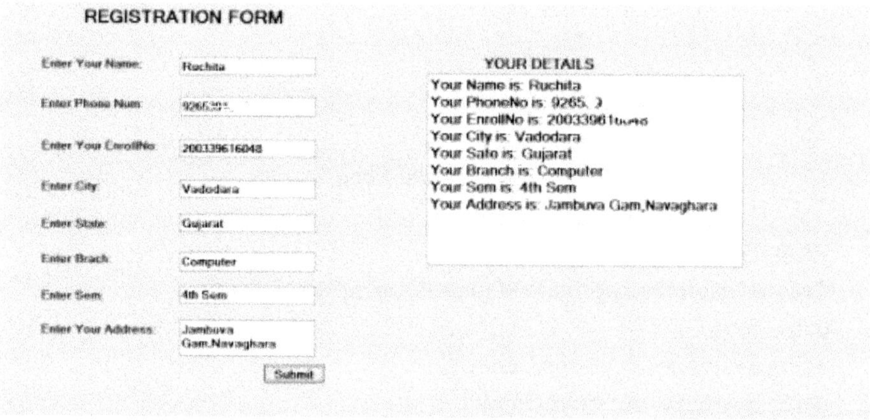

Output of Prog. 4

PRACTICAL 5:

Create windows application to use the Timer Control.

```
using System;
using System.Collections.Generic;
using System.ComponentModel;
using System.Data;
using System.Drawing;
using System.Linq;
using System.Text;
using System.Windows.Forms;
namespace PRATICAL_10
{
public partial class frmalarm : Form
{
```

```
public frmalarm()
{
InitializeComponent();
}
private void timer1_Tick(object sender, EventArgs e)
{
label1.Text = DateTime.Now.ToString();
}
private void btnstart1_Click(object sender, EventArgs e)
{
timer1.Start();
}
private void btnstop_Click(object sender, EventArgs e)
{
timer1.Stop();
}
}
}
```

OUTPUT:

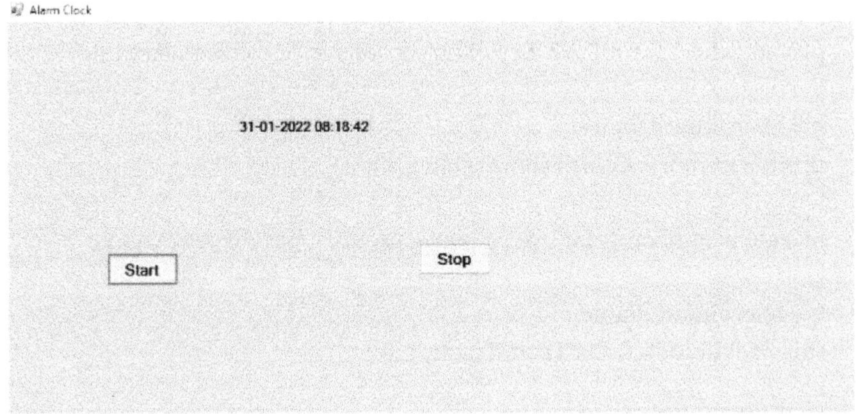

Output of Prog. 5

PRACTICAL 6:

Create windows application to use Picture Box Control.

```
using System;
```

```
using System.Collections.Generic;
using System.ComponentModel;
using System.Data;
using System.Drawing;
using System.Linq;
using System.Text;
using System.Windows.Forms;
namespace PRACTICAL_11
{
public partial class frmScroll : Form
{
int r = 0, g = 0, b = 0;
public frmScroll()
{
InitializeComponent();
}
private void hScrollBar1_Scroll(object sender, ScrollEventArgs e)
{
r = hScrollBar1.Value;
this.BackColor = Color.FromArgb(r, g, b);
}
private void hScrollBar2_Scroll(object sender, ScrollEventArgs e)
{
g = hScrollBar2.Value;
this.BackColor = Color.FromArgb(r, g, b);
}
private void hScrollBar3_Scroll(object sender, ScrollEventArgs e)
{
b = hScrollBar2.Value;
this.BackColor = Color.FromArgb(r, g, b);
}
}
}
```

OUTPUT:

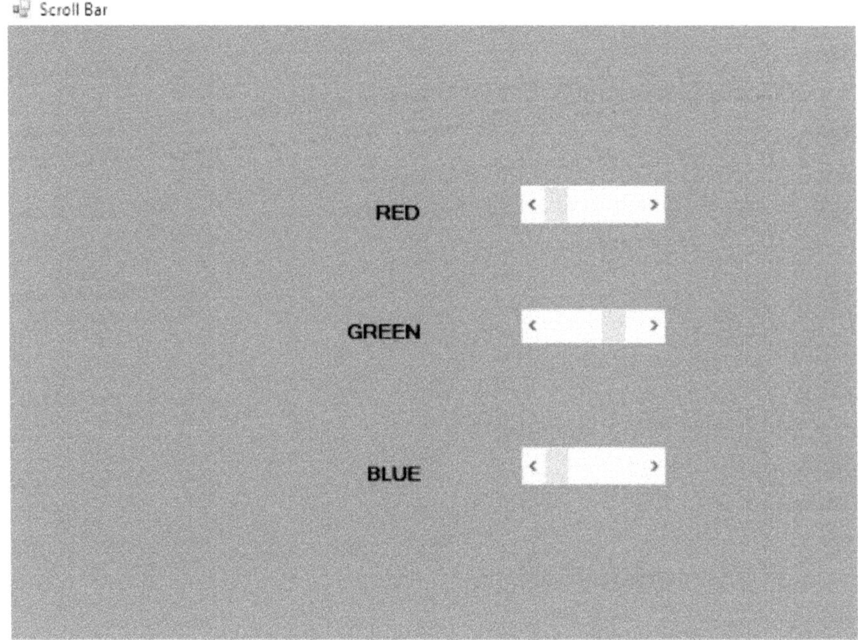

Output of Prog. 6

PRACTICAL 7:

Write C# Program Switch Case.

```
using System;
using System.Collections.Generic;
using System.Linq;
using System.Text;
namespace Switchcase
{
class Program
{
static void Main(string[] args)
{
int day;
Console.Write(&quot;Enter between 1 to 7 to display
day&quot;);
day = int.Parse(Console.ReadLine());
```

```
switch (day)
{
case 1:
Console.WriteLine(&quot;Today is Sunday&quot;);
break;
case 2:
Console.WriteLine(&quot;Today is Monday&quot;);
break;
case 3:
Console.WriteLine(&quot;Today is Tuesday&quot;);
break;
case 4:
Console.WriteLine(&quot;Today is
Wednesday&quot;);
break;
case 5:
Console.WriteLine(&quot;Today is
Thursday&quot;);
    break;
case 6:
Console.WriteLine(&quot;Today is Friday&quot;);
break;
case 7:
Console.WriteLine(&quot;Today is
Saturday&quot;);
break;
default:
Console.WriteLine(&quot;Please Enter Proper
Day&quot;);
break;
}
Console.ReadLine();
}
}
}
```

OUTPUT:

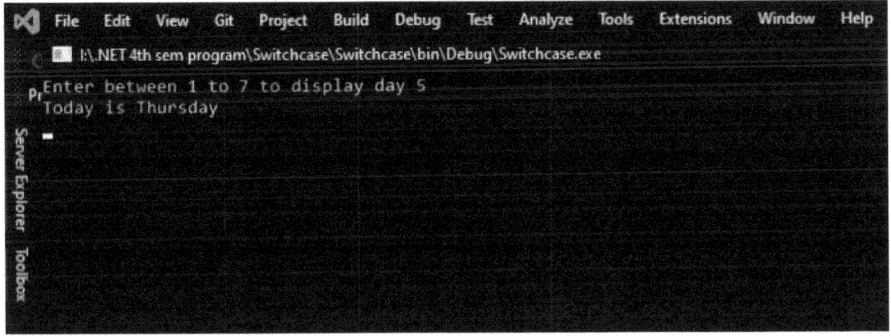

Output of Prog. 7

PRACTICAL 8:

Write C# Program Switch Case.

```
using System;
using System.Collections.Generic;
using System.ComponentModel;
using System.Data;
using System.Drawing;
using System.Linq;
using System.Text;
using System.Windows.Forms;
namespace PRATICAL_12
{
public partial class Form1 : Form
{
Image File;
public Form1()
{
InitializeComponent();
}
private void pictureBox1_Click(object sender,
EventArgs e)
{
}
private void button1_Click(object sender,
EventArgs e)
```

```
{
pictureBox1.BackgroundImage =
Image.FromFile(@&quot;C:\Users\admin\Desktop\1234.jpeg&quot;);
}
private void btnsave_Click(object sender,
EventArgs e)
{
SaveFileDialog S = new SaveFileDialog();
    S.Filter = &quot;JPEG (* .jpeg) | (*.JPEG)&quot;;
if (S.ShowDialog()==DialogResult.OK)
{
File.Save(S.FileName);
}
}
private void btnOPEN_Click_1(object sender,
EventArgs e)
{
SaveFileDialog F = new SaveFileDialog();
F.Filter = &quot;(*.jpg;*.jpeg;.*.gif;
*.jfif;)|*.jpg;*.jpeg;.*.gif.*.jfif&quot;;
if (F.ShowDialog() == DialogResult.OK)
{
File = Image.FromFile(F.FileName);
pictureBox1.Image = File;
}
}
private void Form1_Load(object sender, EventArgs
e)
{
}
private void progressBar2_Click(object sender,
EventArgs e)
{
int i;
progressBar1.Minimum = 0;
progressBar1.Maximum = 250;
for (i = 0; i &lt;= 250; i++)
{
```

```
progressBar1.Value = i;
}}}}
```

OUTPUT:

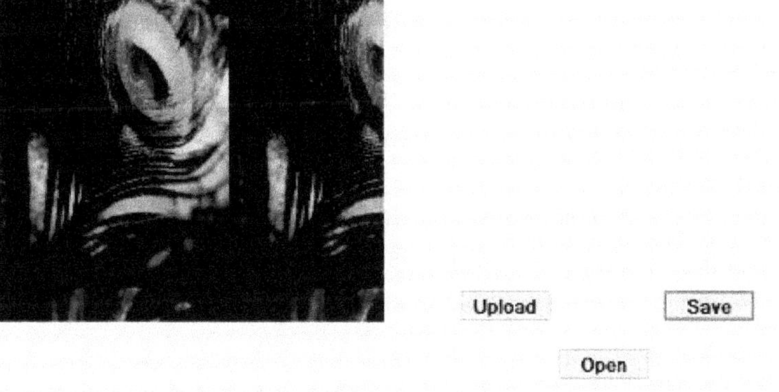

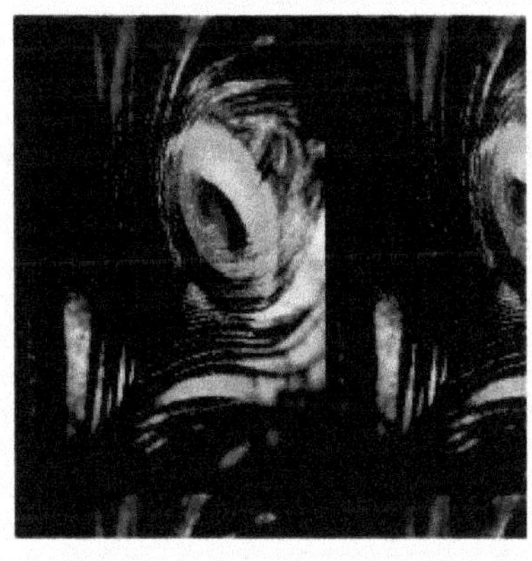

Output of Prog. 8

PRACTICAL 9:

Write a windows application to display the records of student in DataGridView control.

```
using System;
using System.Collections.Generic;
using System.ComponentModel;
using System.Data;
using System.Drawing;
using System.Linq;
using System.Text;
using System.Windows.Forms;
using System.Data.SqlClient;
namespace WindowsFormsApplication1
{
public partial class Form2 : Form
{
```

```
public Form2()
{
InitializeComponent();
}
    private void button1_Click(object sender, EventArgs e)
{
SqlConnection conn = new SqlConnection(@&quot;Data
Source=.\SQLEXPRESS;AttachDbFilename=&quot;C:\Users\Brijesh\
Documents\Visual Studio
2008\ListBox\WindowsFormsApplication1\WindowsFormsApplication1\
Database1.mdf&quot;;Integr
ated Security=True;User Instance=True&quot;);
string str=&quot;Selct * from student &quot;;
conn .Open ();
SqlCommand cmd=new SqlCommand (str ,conn );
SqlDataAdapter ad=new SqlDataAdapter (str ,conn );
    .Net Programming Lab (03606260)
    PPI Page 39
DataSet ds=new DataSet();
DataTable dt;
ad.Fill (ds,&quot;std&quot;);
dt=ds.Tables [&quot;student&quot;];
dataGridView1 .DataSource =dt;
}}}
```

OUTPUT:

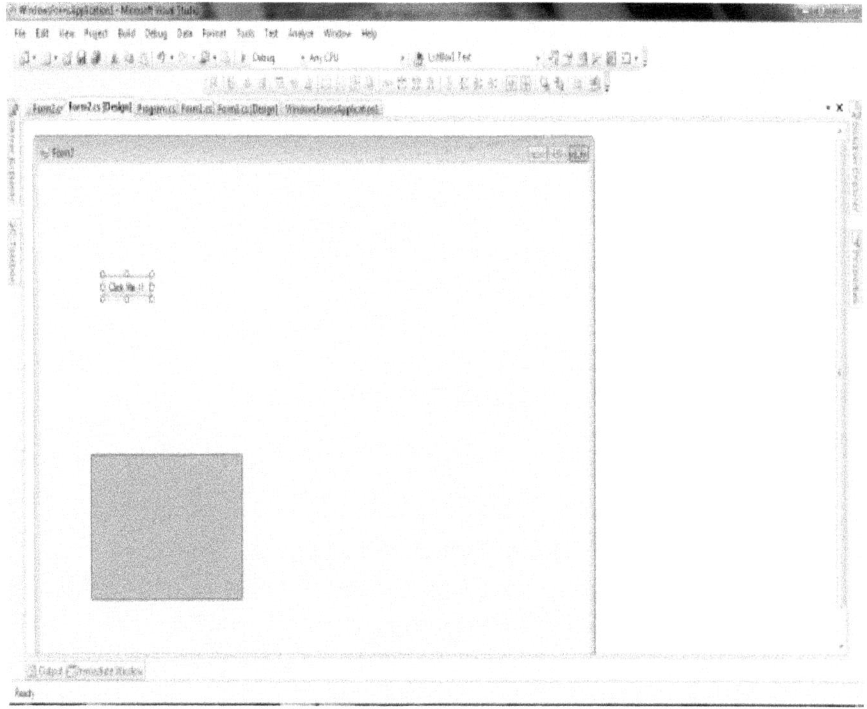

Output of Prog. 9

PRACTICAL 10:

Write a windows application to display InputBox.

In C#.Net you are not able to add input box but after adding the reference of Vb.Net You can use input box in exiting c#.net application.To add the reference follow above steps given in input box question.

```
using System;
using System.Collections.Generic;
using System.ComponentModel;
using System.Data;
using System.Drawing;
using System.Linq;
using System.Text;
using System.Windows.Forms;
using Microsoft.VisualBasic;
namespace Input_Message_Box
```

```
{
public partial class Form1 : Form
{
public Form1()
{
InitializeComponent();
}
private void Form1_Load(object sender, EventArgs
e)
{
}
private void button1_Click(object sender,
EventArgs e)
{
int a,b,c;
a=int.Parse(Interaction.InputBox(&quot;Input First
Value&quot;,&quot;1st Value&quot;,&quot;Enter Interger Value&quot;,-1, -1));
b=int.Parse(Interaction.InputBox(&quot;Input First
Value&quot;,&quot;2nd Value&quot;,&quot;Enter Interger Value&quot;,-1,
-1));
c=a+b;
// String msg = &quot;Demo&quot;;
// String title = &quot;prg&quot;;
    //MessageBox.Show(msg, title);
MessageBox.Show(c.ToString(),&quot;Addition of 2
Values&quot;, Buttons.OKCancel, MessageBoxIcon.Information);
// MessageBox.Show(&quot;GOOD MORNING...\nHERE CLICK
FOR INFORMATION\n&quot;, MessageBoxButtons.OKCancel);
// MessageBox.Show (&quot;Last day for your &quot;);
}}}
```

OUTPUT:

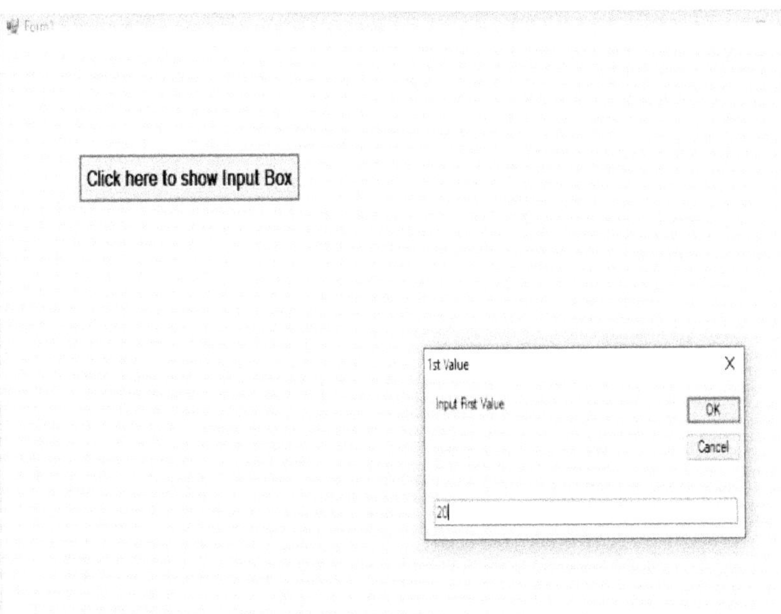

Output of Prog. 10

www.ingramcontent.com/pod-product-compliance
Ingram Content Group UK Ltd.
Pitfield, Milton Keynes, MK11 3LW, UK
UKHW022013190726
13853UKWH00005B/1913